Life as I know it

Ziana Singh

BookLeaf Publishing

Presentation by *BookLeaf Publishing*

Web: www.bookleafpub.com

E-mail: info@bookleafpub.com

ISBN: 9789357211116

First edition 2022

Presentation by *BookLeaf Publishing*

Web: www.bookleafpub.com

E-mail: info@bookleafpub.com

ISBN: 9789357211116

First edition 2022

DEDICATION

To my family – Smiggles, Dad and Mum.

And my best friends who I love to bits.

ACKNOWLEDGEMENT

Just a little note to thank my publishers for the opportunity that I have been waiting for…

Special thanks to all the big people in my life who motivated me the whole way through…

PREFACE

It was around 5 years ago, when I first realised that putting words to paper makes them come alive. It was at this time when one of my friends left, which made me write her one of my first poems. Since then, I have been inspired to continue my quest and dreams to become an author, penning down not only stories, but poems and random scribbles that cross my mind…

This dream has and will continue to follow me as I grow up. Writing is my passion and it is my pleasure to be able to now share this experience with some of you. Hope you enjoy my first book – hopefully first of many!

Once

Once there was a train,
That had a smart brain,

Once there was a laugh,
That gave out autographs,

Once there was a sail
That was covered in Sea Snails,

Once there was a ceiling,
That had strange feelings,

Once there was a witch,
Who loved to snitch,

Once there was a pot,
That was always full of snot,

Once there was a talking tree,
That sat down next to me,
We talked and talked all day,
Till we had no more to say…

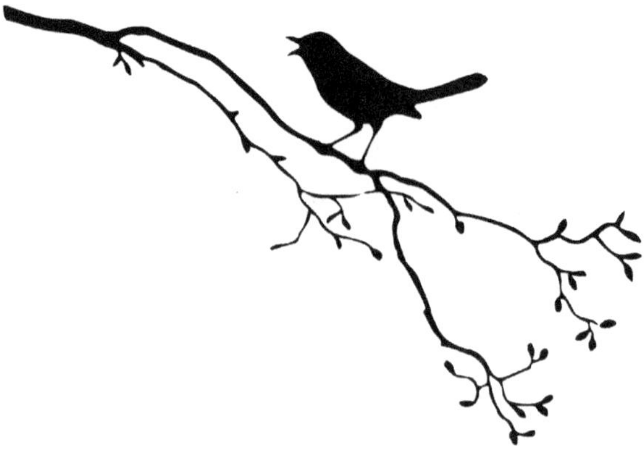

My Troublesome Sister

My troublesome sister,
Had a mister
Who bossed her every day!
No matter how many times she says
He simply just won't go away!

He follows her 'round,
Wherever she goes
Won't stop for the sound
Of a small doze.

Then one day, finally at last!
She turned around to say, real fast,
"I'm tired of you being here!"
She said, as she saw him wipe a tear,
"Plus, I need to go college!
With learning, I will gain more knowledge;
Summaries, passages, interesting facts,
All for English and my acts."

She turned, suddenly shy,
She didn't want him to see her cry!
Hands ready, face of despair, she ran back home.
My troublesome sister
And her mister
Were suddenly both on their own.

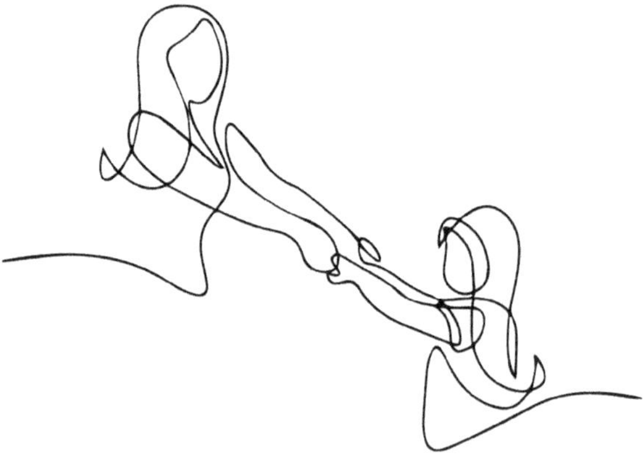

Pip

Pip
Pip pup
Pip pup pow
The cat goes meow

Pip
Pip parp
Pip Park poink
The pig goes oink

Pip
Pip plip
Pip plip pawk
The toucan goes squawk

Pip
Pip plee
Pip plee paa
The monkey goes ooh ooh ahah

Pip
Pip pop
Pip pop pru
The cow goes moo

Pip
Pip pro
Pip pro praa
The sheep goes baaa

Pip
Pip pil
Pip pil poo
The rooster goes cockadoodledoo!

Pip
Pip pip
Pip pip pap
The dog goes yap

Pip pip pip
Pips all around
Always found
But what about the other sounds
All in the dark
Never leave a mark
Ready to be read
Ready to be said!!

Hay fever Season

I have a big fear…
The hay fever season's here!

It starts with a sneeze;
Achoo !! achooooo!
Our noses freeze
And EVERYONE'S blue!

It starts with a tickle,
Proceeding to a sniffle,
Laugh, smirk giggle and scoff
But even I have a bad cough!

It starts with your nose all red,
Next thing you know
You're sick in bed!
Not to go out
No more to be said!

It starts with the eyes,
Oh, I wish they dry!
With it always watering
I'm always faltering!

But the worst is dad,
I'm just glad
I'm not as sick as him.
After all its quite grim,
to be in bed all the time.

And – uh oh!
He's gonna blow!
here comes the bomb…
everyone stays calm!
Dad's gonna sneeze!

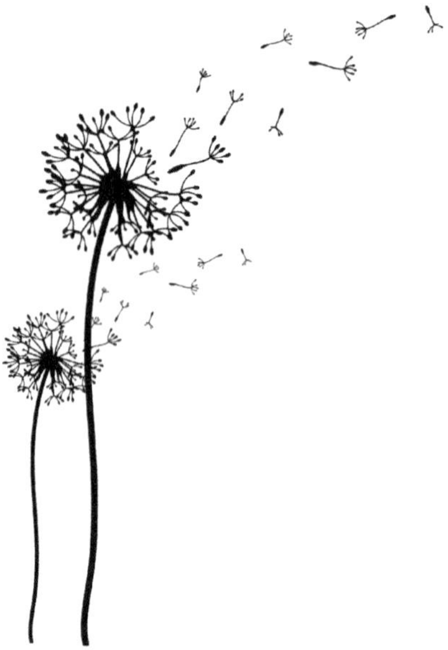

Magic in the Air

The day has passed.
Quick, go fast!
Have a peek around the door
Go on, explore!
Run, run!
Here they come!
A pixie, a dwarf, a bear, a fairy,
A soldier, a cannon, the little lamb and Mary
A unicorn, an Ogre and a Troll,
A racket, a football and a goal
All of them sprouting little arms and legs,
And a lovely cute face that really did beg!

Supporting a line behind one another
In front of them - a giant fother!
Jumping in one by one
God, that would weight a ton!
Slowly it rolls away,
Like a mini-Santa's sleigh!

A door then (magically) appears,
In they go, them and their peers,
Into an unknown world we never knew was
here.

Follow them in, don't be shy,
Otherwise, you'll never know why...

Inside is a beautiful land,
Like a beach covered in sand!
Almost too good to be true,
As whatever you see you could chew!
A truly edible paradise,
I mean, how nice!

Suddenly all goes black,
And a snap you're back.
Your teacher in front of you,
And you in a deep doo doo…

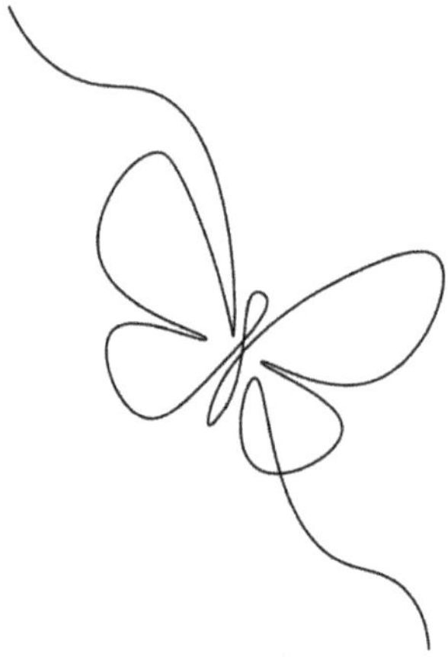

Paradise

The sound of gentle breeze,
Goodness knows how many degrees,
The waves ever so calm and cool,
Much better than the swimming pool.

Follow the waves,
Swim with the dolphins,
Go be brave,
You'll see it was fun!

See how they sell,
Pretty sea shells,
Buy one or two,
Paint them blue,
Just like the sea,
And be free...

The palm trees and the coconuts,
Go lovely with a few nuts,
Succulent, sweet – a great desire,
A must-need-a true attire.

The palm trees and the coconuts,
Go lovely with a few nuts,
Succulent, sweet – a great desire,
A must-need-a true attire.

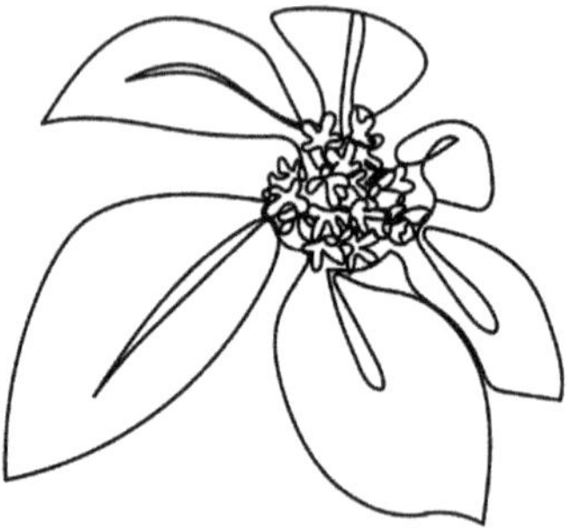

Dreams

Can you see him?
There, that boy?
No ‘course you can’t,
But – I can.
And if you could,
You would see some clouds,
Pink, red, orange – all sorts,
Just above his head.
Well, those are dreams.
And the colours?
You could say they’re feelings;
For example, the red ones are nightmares-
Those I keep with a label.
Keep closed,
Dangerous if exposed.
With labels, I tend to rhyme.
(or the note won’t stick to the jar)
Or the yellow ones!
Those are disgusting!
It doesn’t need a label,
As they look like a vomit!
They always make me feel nauseous.
Then there are pink ones-
Those need to be kept in a locked jar!
Its love.

And can grow very strong...
The orange ones are happy dreams,
And can be kept wild and free,
As they don't do much harm.
(Damage however "sigh!")
The green ones are for adventure,
They allow you to go anywhere,
But often distract you.
So I keep them in an opaque jar.
The blue ones are flying.
(Practically anywhere in the sky)
However, if you're on a plane,
And you get sick on them,
You would probably have bits of both blue and yellow.

Purple, is for the sea,
Like you're on the beach,
Or a mermaid,
(that would need orange too).

Indigo is for sad dreams,
Any sad thing really,
And what makes me sad?
Well, there are so many indigos
In this world!
I have 3,478 jars of them
(and counting!)
I make sure all dreams are safe,

And maybe one day,
Just maybe -
I’ll come to your house
Just to collect your special dreams…

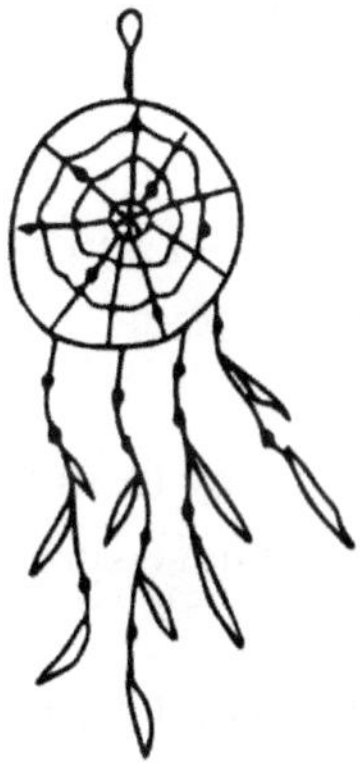

Flying

Flying High,
In the sky,
Like a bird,
With no blizzards.

No rain,
Nothing to gain,
Flying alone,
Though I'm not gonna moan.

Too good to be true
And the best thing is – I don't Coo!
Even Better, Food is free!

Pizza, sausages, Honey fresh from a bee!
All of them seem to have sprouted tiny, baby wings,
Some aren't so keen on heights – instead, they have springs!

Catch them, eat them!
But now an unknown ache occurs..
I’ve fallen of the bed and my back now hurts!

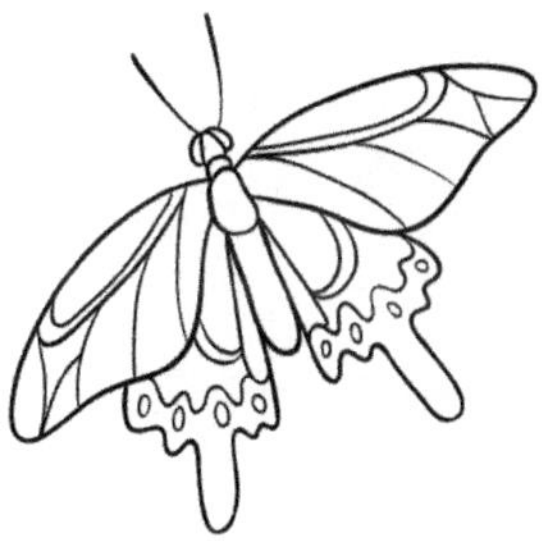

What am I

Shiny and sparkling,
A glistening white,
Light dancing upon it,
A bright hot pink beside it.

Small gaps in the middle of each,
Covered by a brilliant pink,
Yet smoother.

It helps you chew,
But you must take care of them,
Or they'll go missing…

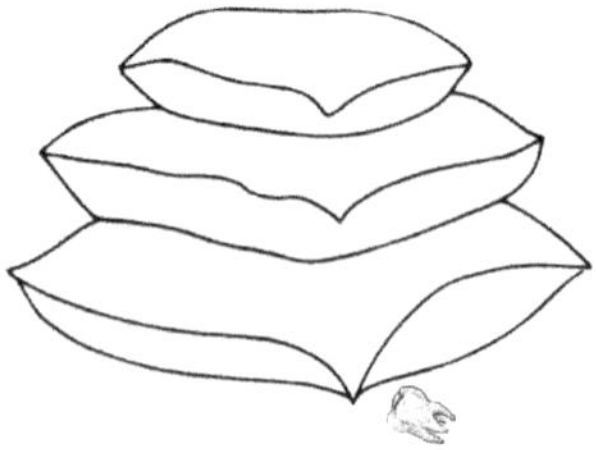

One Smile

Once a boy from quite unknown,
Gave me a gift.
A brilliant smile to light my day,
That really did lift,
My heart and my soul,
I passed it to all that came.
It was a very good gift
That I passed back to him.

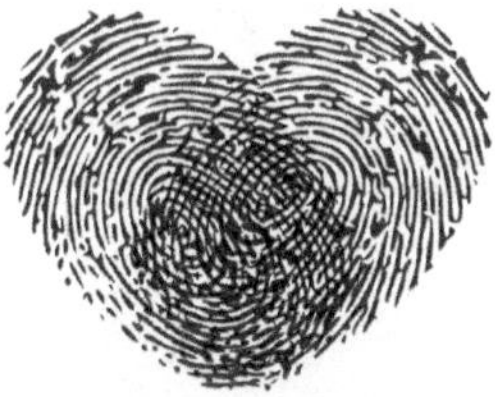

Try your best

Try your best,
First get rest.
Reach for the stars,
Go further than mars,
Never be afraid,
If you failed.

The only way to learn,
Is to fail.
Though it will burn,
It will help you set sail.

Its easy to give up;
But don't, just have a break.
Try your best to get up,
But you don't have to do it for your sake.

Your friends will be there,
Right by your side.
Such loyalty is rare,
And they will be there to guide.

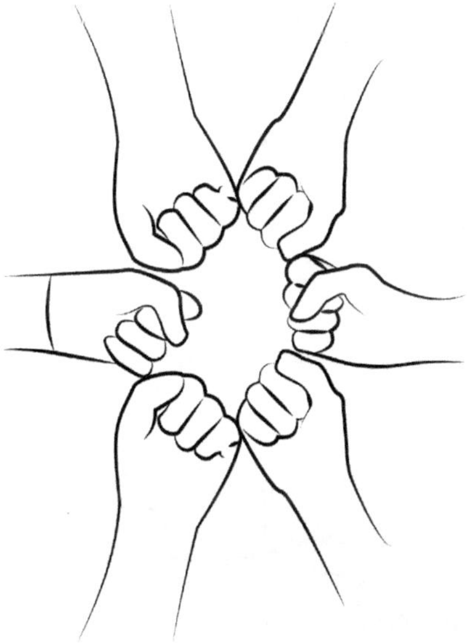

The Creaks of the night

It was the dead of night.
I was hungry,
So I crept downstairs.
Creeeaaaaak……

The stairs had never made a sound before.
I walked faster.
Creeeeeeeaaak… Creeeeaaaaaak…
Creeeeeeeaaaak….

The stairs never seemed to stop.
Round and round it went,
I started to feel dizzy.
Then everything went black,
And I was black and blue!

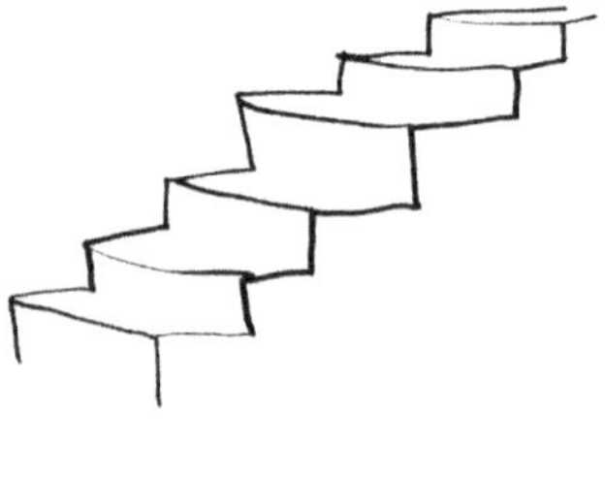

The way to school

My house is far away,
From my school and its driveway,
Its impossible to go to and from,
That too for a full term!

First you get out of the house-
Easy you say?
As easy as catching a brainy dormouse
- They always get away!

The reason why its so hard,
- Its covered in magic ivy!
Like glitter on a shiny card,
But more uglier and mighty!

The moment you step out,
The vines reach out to grab you.
And (most likely) without a doubt,
You're upside down – its true!

But there is one itsy, bitsy fault,
Our ivy gets flattered with ease.
So when it's about to assault,

Whisper a compliment – watch it laugh and wheeze.

Gives you time to rush right past,
And you've passed the first task at last!

The second task,
Is simpler than the last,
You have to cross a bridge.

A bridge is there as there is a moat,
But underneath is a fire breathing goat!

You need to give it a decent fee,
Then you must quickly flee.
A fee and perhaps a tip,
And don't show him a lower lip!

And before you know it,
You're ready to quit!
But don't lose hope,
You CAN cope!
As you've cleared the second task!

The third task is the hardest of all – scarier than a bloodshot ghoul,
Scarier than anything…
Surviving a day at school!!!!

Well done Jacob, good effort, but I'm going to have to give you an F! This has nothing to do with your Maths essay! See me after class.
Mrs Jenifer

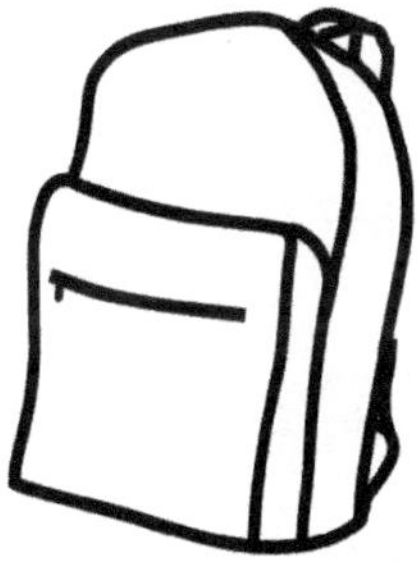

The UMO

I was hungry.
I bit into a snack-an apple.
Chomp, mmm juicy!
Another bite,
Real good!
Hang on…
I never knew that inside of an apple was red!

I put my hand around my mouth,
Gasping in surprise.
I looked at my hands
-Blood red!
I looked at the apple again,
Ahaa. Finally!
A white piece!
But its sticking out.
So I pulled it,
And I yanked it,
And after many efforts,
It came out.

My mouth has stopped bleeding now.
I inspected the white thing.
It was a UMO!
An unidentified mouth Object!!

I went around screaming,
Help.. help!
A UMO!

The postman joined in,
Help Help! a UMO!

Then the taxi driver,
Help! Help a UMO!

Soon we were all tired of running.
So we stopped by a shop called
Marys mirror.

I looked inside.
Hundreds of me!! Staring right back at me!
I smiled.
The hundreds of me smiled too.

Suddenly I saw a black tooth...

I ran out to the dentist,
"Can you fix my tooth?"
Except it sounded like,
"Can too ficks my tooth?"
The dentist laughed,
"That's no problem!
Its perfect and fine!
You've just lost a tooth!"

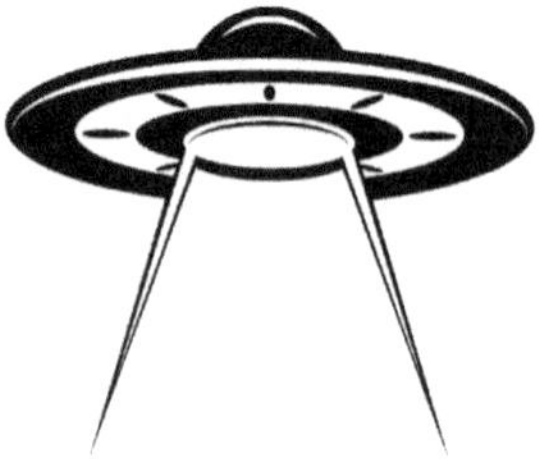

Homework

The joys of school,
Are brilliant and cool,
Break time drama,
With the usual karma.

PE and Art,
Making the teacher fart,
Playing brand new pranks,
Not saying please and thanks.
Always breaking the rules,
Yet still the teachers' jewels!

End of the day,
One thing left to say,
HOMEWORK!
Is it dreadful spellings?
Or could it be maths?
Whatever it is, watch out!
I like it? I seriously doubt it!

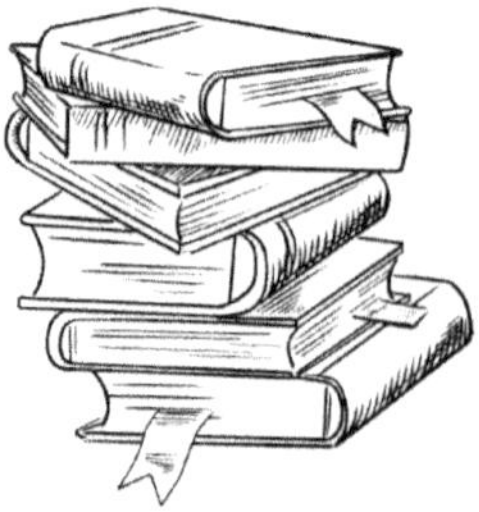

Chilli

Makes your mouth burn all over,
Nothing will work – not even clover!

Makes the mouth fire,
Yet the spice will never tire!

Makes it hurt so much,
Even the lightest touch
Makes it red and puffy,
Not at all a toughie!

Makes it hot, hot, hot!
Hot – I never forgot!

But look! firemen to save the day!
Yet still at the fridge, so far away!

Come on, get up!
You can do it!

Milk has never tasted better!

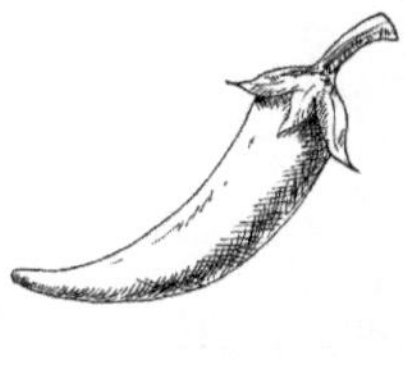

Dads

Everyone knows mums are better than dads.

Dads make you work,

Mums bake you cookies.

Dads get angry when

You're covered in mud.

Mums love when you're having fun!

But what's worst?

Dads are ready to kill you after they've...

Seen your report card!

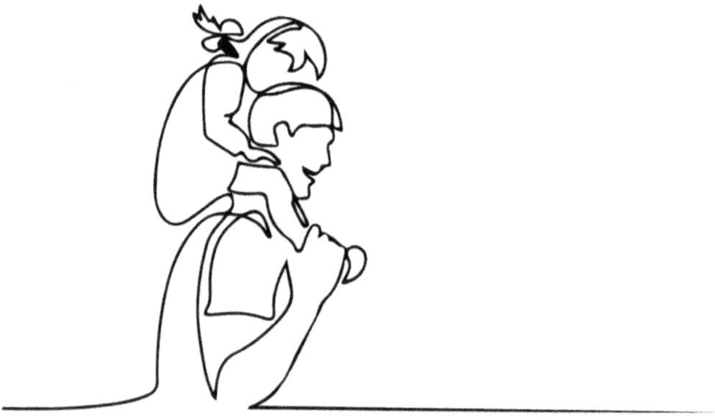

Pixie Jokes

Nights are just the simple starts,
of Pixies playing the jokes.
and (don't ask me why) collecting things in carts!
making them yawn,
making them snore,
much louder than a sleeping boar.
making them grizzle and grunt,
to them, its an extreme stunt.
Making them talk yapping all night,
Imagine the sound they'd make in a fight!
Making them uncomfortable,
Tossing and turning.
What would parents would say?
'a waste if time – you could've been learning!'
Making them sleepwalk for hours on end,
Making them yawn if they ever bend!
So next time you're dozing off,
Careful of the pixie's jokes!

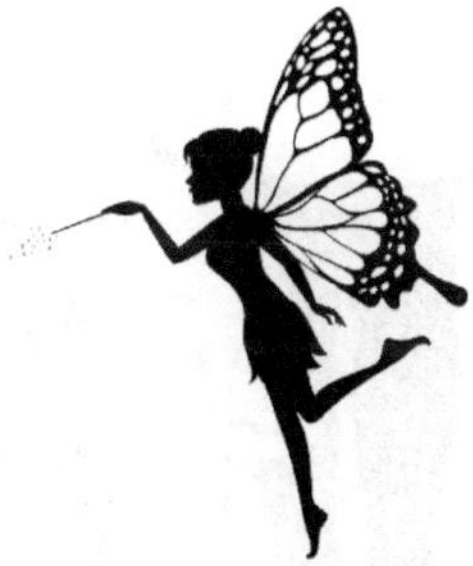

A New Start

The time has come near,
And a new door opens,
Make new friends,
Don't be afraid,
Have no fear,
But remember the memories,
From the past,
The games we played,
In the same class every year,
One of the first few friends,
Never to be forgotten.

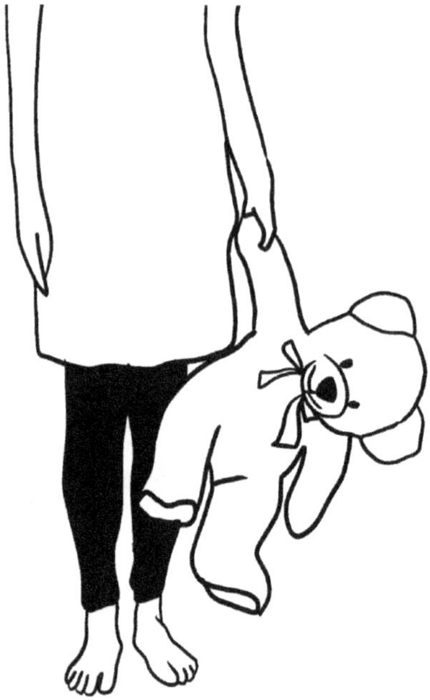

Shattered

Shattered down to the ground,
Got nothing else to do.
I walked into the future,
I saw you running down,
You were shattered, shattered down to the
ground.
You had nothing, nothing else to do,
So I helped you up, but you wanted to be alone.

My heart will shine,
To the pressure above,
When I walk into the future…

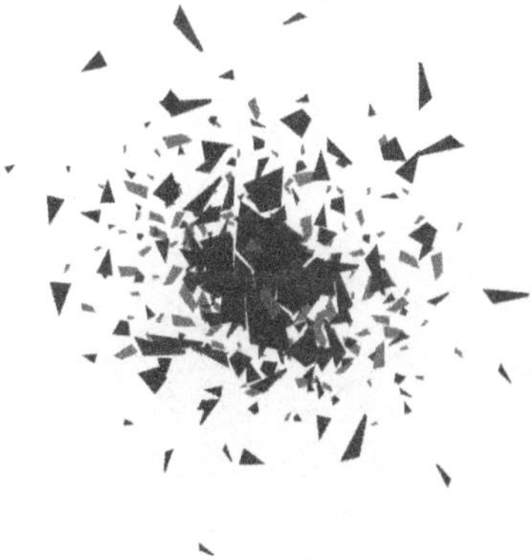

The Magic Box

I will put in the box:
The vibrant colours of a soaring rainbow,
The mysterious fog surrounding me
Like a shadowy creature,
The wild tornado swirling
Like spiteful candyfloss
Across the land.

I will put in the box,
The upturning tsunami,
Sloshing thought the drowning windows,
The ferocious lighting,
Stabbing the terrified earth,
The pounding rain drumming gently on rooftops.

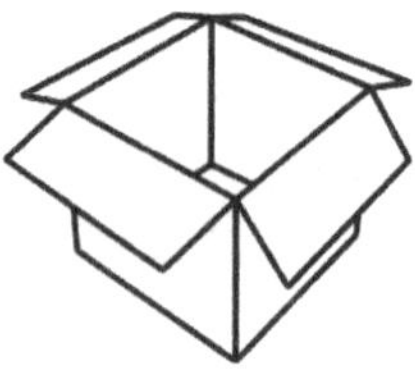

www.ingramcontent.com/pod-product-compliance
Lightning Source LLC
Chambersburg PA
CBHW051744130826
49812CB00033B/1000
* 9 7 8 9 3 5 7 2 1 1 1 1 6 *